I0202609

Point No Point

Molly Mattfield Bennett

FUTURECYCLE PRESS
www.futurecycle.org

Library of Congress Control Number: 2016943285

Copyright © 2016 Molly Mattfield Bennett
All Rights Reserved

Published by FutureCycle Press
Lexington, Kentucky, USA

ISBN 978-1-942371-07-6

For Sheldon

Contents

One

Two

Three

Four

Five

Six

One

Out of the Long Silence

The bell swings in the stone tower, sound rings out over the upturned
heads of the watchers, swirls in wide circles of deranged pigeons,
echoes off walls and rubble, floods dazed ears.
There is no escape from clang and
clang except the delusion that all is well, that here
people make love and laugh, that fields do not flood or cities
drown, that the people's cries do not reverberate within the bell's peal.

***

They left home—crossed land and sea
promised to their god,
each other

They came burdened with boxes
of expectation
their trunks overflowed with fragments

They eked out a bare
hard-scrabble life
on the thin strip between sea and forest

But the wilderness loomed, and they were haunted
by those who track
wild animals and live out in sun and storm

Evenings within the candle's reach they tell of the fierce journey

Others cross checkpoints, seas
on anything
that might float not sink

by the wisp of a prayer
they slip through
cracks

Here
they stumble
unable

to speak
the language
eat

the food
laugh
at the jokes

They seek out
shops
on back streets

hunt spices
bundles of dried herbs
and fish

They huddle
in borrowed rooms
to recreate

the subtle taste
of memory
and tell of the journey

Here nothing is firm or clear
the sea scours the sand beneath our feet.

The Course of Empire: A Series of Paintings
by Thomas Cole (1834-1836)

The Savage State

It is dawn. Wild dark clouds, fog in the air swirls; mauve to pink
encircles the crag and boulder. Within the primeval forest
there are graceful deer, stalked by a hunter with bow and arrow; across
the water in a clearing is an encampment of tepees. After the storm
it is bright on the horizon, the air clean.

The Arcadian-Pastoral State

The crag and boulder rise clear in the soft air; pastel clouds trail.
On a hill, Stonehenge circles a fire and, in the May wood, girls
flow in dance. There are goats and sheep grazing, no wild animals or
birds; a man traces geometric shapes in the dirt and a boy draws
the figure of a man on the stone bridge.

The Consummation of Empire

In the noonday light, the crag and boulder are sharp against the blue
sky. All is gilded spectacle—Greco-Roman-Egyptian glory—
with carved ships on elaborate waterways; fountains splash. There are
elephants and horses, slender columns; the people crowd on
every ledge, road to the summit. The city is a festival of artifice.

Destruction

Beyond the crag and boulder is a pale patch of sky; clouds loom over
the waves, threaten the city. Soldiers wield axes; bodies
are slashed, raped, tossed on the marble steps. They fall from the
walls, balconies and ships. There are fires.
In the city there are no birds or animals; the people die.

Desolation

End of day—the crag and boulder are stark in a sky; there are wisps
of clouds, a calm moon with perhaps a face.
The sun slants. Here, on a fragment of a column, a black lizard clings;
on its broken top, a black crane sits on a stick nest
and another wades at water's edge. There are no people.

The Course of Empire: A Collage of Images
by Molly Mattfield Bennett (2014)

It is bright after the storm—there are deer, a slant of sun—a lizard
clings; cranes wade. People crowd to the summit. Goats and sheep...
jets target militant hideouts—a boy draws—it is dawn—
a whirl, dark fog... Bodies *at least 50 killed early Sunday.* They fall
from walls, balconies.... There are fires.
The crag and boulder are stark in blue sky—
Politician shot dead in Kosovo, his hometown... his spiked hair—
there are wisps of clouds and perhaps a moon.
Soldiers wield axes... *we cannot collect our bodies
from the debris....* grey sky...clouds...loom...the people die in
Pakistan, the West Bank, Syria...mass execution of Iraqi soldiers...
It is dawn, the end of day...on the horizon, the air clean...
clouds...threaten the city—
*In Chak Chak, Iran—means drip, drip—Zoroastrians celebrate...
the spring slowly drips from the ceiling
as the mountain sheds tears in remembrance of Nikbanou who
sheltered there.*

(Quotations from the *Boston Globe* article "The World,"
Monday, June 16, 2014, appear in italics.)

New Bedford

On Johnny Cake Hill, the Seamen's Bethel is marked by death

> *John Talbot*
> *Who at the age of 18, was lost overboard*
> *Near the Isle of Desolation, off Patagonia*
> *Nov. 1st 1836*

> *Captain Ezekiel Hardy*
> *Who in the bow of his boat was killed by a*
> *Sperm whale on the coast of Japan*
> *Aug. 3rd 1833*

At sea the wind changes, here markers sink in dust.

An immense forest of ships once rode the tide, clanked
against the docks, one another and the wind
blew salt fish over the city.

Now tourists come, collect stories of long whaling voyages,
of textiles shipped round the world
and of vanished cod. They walk the beach

After storms the tide wrack is thick with shells in seaweed,
plastic bottles, rings tangled in seaweed
and the coiled egg cases of whelks

Within paper walls whole shells hard to see in sand.

(Quotations from Chapter 7 of *Moby Dick* appear in italics.)

Two

Day to Day

Red—

Not the blood of true-love's heart; not granny's pin cushion;
not a frog in the Amazon; not M&S Auto Body; not the rose
in all the poems; not the Subway Line; not velvet cake; not
mid-scream's angry face; but

Red—the sun rises out of the sea. A grey bird calls to a far off plane.
His streaming repertoire of chirps, ring-tones, songs spiral; a silver
streak over white clouds; as if he dares the plane to sing.

Petals swirl. Begin. Sweep the floor, wash the dishes. Confetti of
cherry drifts over the sill; grasp the straw broom, the dish cloth,
and see the wood of the floor, the bowls in the water.

Breathe. A man runs his dogs on the beach, builds his house of found
wood. Board by board the design holds, keeps out
the wind and rain; clouds scud on the harbor.

Yellow—

Not ripe lemons, or the yolk of an egg; not slang for coward;
not a species of Flicker or wading bird; not the enraged wasp
caught in cypress, pine or poplar; but

Yellow—the dandelions, gold circles amid bitter leaves, milk-white
sap, idle summer's day, curl green stalks; brew wine, the harvest of
sunlight; gone-to-seed puffs blow on the wind.

The flotsam that grows on the verges. Water drips from scrub pine,
witch grass. Dancing in the dunes, a boy tossed driftwood to
the others by the fire. They beat him, just to see him cry.

Where are the burnt ants, the wingless birds?
Under the cellar-hole stairs where the kittens mew.
Only the old and the dogs can hear them.

Blue—

> *Not sad or dreary; not Bluebeard or bottle, bell, blood, bird*
> *or devils; not the music from the grass or mountain ridge; not*
> *a surprise or the unknown; not a color of the moon; but*

Blue—the swallows' wing; the lady who walks the cinder paths; the
children's cries over the grass of *Mother may I?*; the moment
between day and night as they freeze in "Statues."

North and South turn round. There is no North Star or moon light or
magic thread; the gathered dark obscures all to shadow shapes;
the children play till the lady leads them home.

They say once she cast a spell with her sad eyes, and changed a girl
into the statue on the grass and that at dusk she dances
on tip-toe forever among the children.

Dream Catcher

Out from sky and clouds tower bells thunder and vibrate. Pigeons fuss,
settle under foot
    on laden carts or stalls of incense, African carvings,
charms. The air is thick with scent of propane
    sticky nuts, barbecue, fried dough.

Apart, within a white tent she sits, draped in Aegean Blue. Her fingers
    loop and twist bright skeins spun from old plastic bags;
    with her hook she catches the day's fragments, fashions
small glitter bags and many-pocketed bags for tools,
    odds and ends of thoughts.

Streets on streets converge.
    In a square "the Child with Bird" fountain splashes,
        the one-man-band clangs and stomps.
Music surges, swells the gaudy parade.

Their tangled lives re-imagined by touch of gauze,
        wisp of lace or feather. They dance
up the subway stairs, startle the puffed pigeons that scatter crumbs
    tossed by a flying child.
Come out, whoever you are. Come.

Dance in the street where the stilt walker struts, doffs his plumed hat
as the puppet heads sing,
    We are your other selves (come with a word of caution)
though you will not dance and make merry
you cannot escape those who roam the night.

Night Visitations

By night the restless come, demand to be heard. They want to be seen
to tell their stories.

        They wait on hard benches. The marble hall echoes,
their words reverberate. A woman flees her past, invents a life
gives gifts to the child she was.

            From deep in the drains
        the midnight voice sings with a bang and rattle of
the lost who pull red-wheeled lives.

             Under the sign of the jukebox they dance
to music no one hears. Hearts break as they whirl
and a paralytic cries.

       One o'clock. Insomniacs pace and a fool sleeps on the steps.

Here pranksters revel. Sounds crash, repel off towers
in a duet of metal on metal squeal and grind.

Silent in the night, lights flash red, green, yellow
             into the room where a woman knits
      (bit by bit the pattern comes together)
Tales of forgotten journeys:
           of camel rides through sand
              of a boy who washed his socks in his hat
as a homesick soldier called *Sui Sui* to the pigs across a far field.

By night moments hold, time is fluid, trembles on the edge.

In the mirror images repeat, slip back and forward
            as voices tell and re-tell their stories
their words flow
       weave snarled thoughts into semblance of sense.

The Air Jumps and Quivers

Moving rhythmically
smoothly down the rows
the sun-warm berries stained my fingers
struck by sky and too bright sun
I rested deep under raspberry canes

Visiting in Masai land I entered her house
we sipped sweet tea, there
a dirt floor and a charcoal brazier for cooking
it was cool out of the sun

In a dry place blazed with light
a campesino picked lemons
for lemonade
under a tree we talked by gestures

On a porch a lone child waited
for bare skin to cool
running in and out
between shade and mid-day sun

In the deep dark within dense shade
the dog lay
damp nose under folded paws
feigning sleep
as opposites converged

Sketches of Kenya

Mzungu, Swahili for Caucasian, means
"One who wanders without purpose."

They walk the edges
of the cities and mountain hollows

the women sweep
the hard-packed dirt of dark, tin-roofed houses

and hang out jeans and shirts on lines or leafy bushes
they walk the edges

and in the markets on street corners
sell mangoes, apples, knobby roots and spices

their hands hold the fearful child
they dream and dance in fuchsia and gold

                                         ***

The power was out as they crossed Nairobi
caught in fog their car lights flickered
on the road and obscure shapes.

Until out of the dark,
light flared
from an open hearth and lanterns swung.

Gathered within the expats laughed, ate grilled antelope,
gazelle and zebra.
They drank and talked through the night:

Of how hard they work and no one understands;
Of the women who clean
how they dress for the long walk home;

Of how awkward it is
to give money for ironed shirts, intricate carvings;
of car troubles, death on the road.

Within the shadowed glow, they drank and talked through the night

***

Angled out over the watering hole
the Ark floats in the tree tops

At sunset tourists gather
with drinks
One at a time
the animals come
Three elephants step from the trees
imperceptibly
they move near the water
for hours they stand
poke the mud, rub backs
shift from foot to foot
Rabbits hop, bushbucks skitter
at the least twitch of air
Cape buffalo bunch
a hyena slinks along the far edge
the buffalo turn and glower
the elephants shift
the hyena vanishes back to the trees

In the quiet there are whispers
footfalls and night passes

***

The bus jounced and jolted as tourists crowded the windows
filmed lions, zebras, bits of sky and glimpsed
the long, white tail of a colobus monkey.
From the trees and along the top of a ruined wall
wild monkeys posed.

They recorded the Masai warrior herding on the median strip
the roadside sellers—with perfect pyramids of fruit,
charcoal, seedlings in plastic bags, roasted corn
and the children who chased the bus—shouted,
Mzungu, Mzungu.

They drove up and over flat rocks, the road like a dry river bed
climbed high out in Masai land. In the distance
a boy watched his sheep and a man walked with his cloak and stick
in the space between sky and grass.
There was grass and more grass.

Under a lone flat-topped tree—benches and a chalkboard
with pen, table, book, written in words and pictures.
The teacher called the children from out of the grass.
In the shadow light they bent their heads, looked away from the eyes
of the *Mzungu.*

***

At Ah'med's gate
over a trash can fire
two Somali, in long soldier coats, keep watch

Come as you are
do not leave your strangeness
at the door

Within the lighted room
he has gathered friends and strangers
to eat his camel stew and talk
we tell our stories as night deepens

He is missing a leg
blown off during peace talks
the air shivers

We try to speak clearly of what is in our hearts
it is painful to listen
closely to other's words
to our own

Late, the watchmen walk us back
through the dark alley

***

Small rocks and stones fit the hand
are good to skip

they are good to hurl at strays
Not so good against guns

We drive through dust over rocks
where weeds do not grow

or birds scratch
Here in the rubble children sleep

A child scuttles
and from the wall flings rocks

In Nairobi the slums are not marked on the map
we hunt for the way back

Behind us they collect rocks

***

What is the voice that calls on the Serengeti
on the great plains—calls
to the birds and the vast herds to migrate?

What is the voice that calls
the alewife—the salmon
to run up river to leap again and again?

What is the voice that calls out
from deep in the land
calls a boy or girl to wander?

What is the voice that calls to those caught
behind walls
and compels them to speak?

News of the Day

Out of sun and shade the patients wait for the young nurse to call
their names. Here among bird-less palms,
they cluster in vast robes or trousers.
    I am tired of people getting sick; any little mistake,
you're going to come down with the virus.

At MGH (Lower Level 3) cancer patients wait; they flip the pages
of *Glamour*, the *Globe*, stare at cell phones, computers,
a golden tree with heart leaves—a woman
      in a turban crumples one,
      No one needs to see that.

A monitor lists wait times, support groups, tai chi, a serenity
garden. Under smiles the air is close—a man taps his computer,
asks a newcomer *How are you doing?* His wife just
      graduated from radiation to surgery,
      and then—*There's a chance.*

The nurse and driver load patients in a cramped van and drive all day.
Stop for a flat in the dark, in the mud and rain.
There's no hope here; Ebola will last...next
3 or 4 months will be worse. I wish
I could do more. It is not easy.

        (Ambulance driver, PBS; quotations from the *New York Times,*
        October 2014, appear in italics.)

Three

Somewhere Between Violence

Amid the grit and grime of the day's chase off the cliff
Wile E. Coyote schemes—Run

A flash of gunfire riddles doors and mows down
the small creatures that hide in brush.

***

The surface of the water ripples to the hummock
where a mallard frets over chicks.

Seen from the beginning, the end can be known.
The old turtle rises.

***

In sync, trucks, cars pass through the mechanical city
breakdowns are few; but

Glass, concrete, steel wear on the heart. A hunter slips
behind birch and hemlock to track wild animals across the hills.

Edge of Town

1

the one who lives out
past the edge
of town

comes and goes
through the blown
sharp grass

as shadows shift
a brown mouse
freezes

crouched
beneath
the rusted truck

it will not die tonight
hunter and hunted
pass

under moonlight
and dry scratch
of oak

2

at the edge of town
they dump
wrecked cars, washers, refuse
of abandoned lives

the children tell
of bodies
buried
deep in salt grass

stories of a pretty girl
and her baby
blood
and a white coffin

3

out past the edge of town
a boy walks
through the still dark train yard

away from the shriek
and grind
of wheels on metal rails

under the iron bridge
to wait
and listen for the morning chorus

of sparrow, starling, jay and crow
as the sun turns the clouds
rose-purple

there in wild sumac
brambles
and witch grass

6 A.M., Near the Bridge

Seaweed, jellyfish
Water—7 feet

White egrets
shadow
edges

Gone-to-seed
wild grasses, pinecones

An almost-not-there
brown rabbit
hops

On a dry stump
a hawk

In one claw a half-
empty
skin

Caught Unaware

Waking on a city street
an old man folded his blanket and aligned the edges

The sight of his careful hands
in the damp air
blew the past over me

Once out with my grandfather fishing
with a line and lead sinker
dropping it through morning mist

Salt water rushing under foot to the sea
as the tide turned
we caught sea robins and seaweed

His hands reeling in
wrapping the wet line round smooth wood
carved for a child's hand

Later in a distant city a poet recited for change
the night air shimmered
as his hands smoothed the wrinkled page

Waking on a city street
I unfold forgotten images and align the edges

She Traveled Light and Fast

1

Did not want to be seen
by the eyes that track each breath and slide
over bare skin.

She hid under long, grey skirts
hands to her mouth, but
still her words flashed, ignited her eyes.

To escape
those who would beat her or love her
she became a shadow.

2

She was a white-winged moth who threw herself
at the screen, again and again she tried
to break through.

With the hawks, she perched on ledges
stared down into air's embrace.
She sought

But did not find that one thing. So as not
to make a mess,
she slit her throat in the bath.

3

Perhaps, if she had slipped between shadows
waded the stream
the hounds would have lost her scent.

In winter a rabbit freezes in snow—white
shades to white. On the ridge a vixen
waits in her den.

Yesterday and tomorrow meet
where the sun streaks the bay—red
on gray waves.

A World of Stars and Snow

Behind arched windows of delicate tracery, behind the opaque glass
grotesque, enormous winged creatures shift from perch
to perch, tumble. Shadows rise to fall.
Here is the boy who fashioned a world of stars and snow, and here
the girl who scaled the scaffold to the top of the steeple.
Here is the ragged man, his chair stuck
in the frost-heaved walk, his blanket deep in slush.

***

Mornings he's propped on his crutches
with cup and sign
     Homeless but not hopeless
We give spare change
for a smile and his words
again and again
he stands and waits without expectation
and we wonder:

Does he know the young man with flowers
who clutches paper petals
and cries, *My mother made them*
if you laugh—I'll kill you

Does he know the woman who screams
Damn you Damn you—She circles
her heaped bags
with quick grabs empties one
Our eyes skitter
afraid she'll ask *What to do?*
afraid she'll fling bag, herself away

Can he clap with the girls on the platform
and sing, *Old lady Mack, Mack*
all dressed in black black

Does he ride late at night
as the man with the guitar plays
a sad song
and a spiky-haired boy and his girl
share chicken bits and fries

Lulled by fretful light and rocking world
time pauses
mellow lights flare off the river
we watch him limp through the gate
and still we want to know what he knows

***

Home is a camp by the rush
of cold water
deep in pines on a dry lake

It is a hard farm
where the wind blasts
dark sunlight

It is a pickup truck in the alley
where a man and a dog
wait and watch

Home is the song in your head
it is the cave under the table
It is the end of day

***

Slowly leaf by leaf
the hesitant breeze turns
the maple silver

Till under a low sky
the wind rips
leaves and flowers

After rain
mud and stones sparkle
as torn branches drip

Into the sun he shuffles
between canvas bags
talking
       It's black days ahead
       with them
       looking out only
       for themselves
       They may think I'm crazy
       going through the trash
       but if you're not working
       you got to do something
       Then again you never know
       what you'll find
He pauses by the struck tree
to fill his bag
with broken sticks

Once in Early Sun

With the ground still damp she rose
to cut winter hay for the proud-necked horse.
Back and forth
the reaper swung clean and straight to the wood.

Here by horse and tree is the delicate reaper—
a wire shape in a tangled field.
left to rust
in a clump of grass.

Knock. Peer through the screen door. Words stick
between tongue and teeth.
Bats under the pitched roof scrabble and slip. Unease
turns over, worries shift.

Four

Altar Rock: One Family's Vietnam (in Four Parts)

Dear Fred:

Mother's love was quick to flare as she caught sight,
caressed the curve of an eggplant
delighted in the crinkle
of tissue-wrapped books or hand-wrought tools
She had the gift of tears—saw death
within the curl of fern, the glint of rain or song
Grief or sorrow in the eyes of any living thing
cut deep, stained her days and nights

Dad had enlisted to protect his mother from a white feather,
the gift of small town fear
He'd gone with a Jewish soldier to a concentration camp
so he'd not bear witness alone
Dad wanted a peaceful life—liked to sit
on the back steps as night fell
to think—see connections between paradoxes
and wait for the stars

That morning at breakfast
I choked
Did not ask
about her bandaged wrists
Did not
want to know
Guessed—it was Vietnam
you gone
But I could not
speak

The Nantucket Visit

They stayed at the Jarrett House—Dad walked quiet streets
smoked his cigar

You and Mother argued favorite books and cooked on your attic stove
Meatloaf and mashed potatoes

Dad said Uncle Paul should be there to mash them
and mix the martinis

***

I see the three of you walk the beach
the sky sharp blue, the wind does not sting

You talk—Mother smokes cigarettes
down to the filter

You and she go round and round
the words make no sense

She cries—curses the war,
the killing

She cannot stop—Dad tries
to hold her

You hunch in the dunes, your long arms
round your knees, watch the waves, the gulls

(Uncle Paul was a WWII POW, Stalag 17b near Kerm, Germany.)

The Departure

The day before spring break
teaching your last classes that were not
known to be the last

Saying good-bye
to the island
forgetting no one

Walking that night out
to the ocean
over the moor to Altar Rock

Through the streets
saying good-bye
to a dog on the corner

You take little—
a jacket, a notebook
You watch

The ferry dock, the gulls
strut and squawk—
the island disappears

You walk by the Charles
 read inscriptions on tombstones
at the Old Corner Book Store—buy *Three Men in a Boat*

THAT NIGHT—AIR FRANCE—TO PARIS

>   (Altar Rock is located at one of the highest points on the
>   island of Nantucket. Although the origin of its name cannot
>   be determined, it likely had both humorous and spiritual
>   significance.)

The Letter Received

What is there:

Dear Mother

When you get this I will have gone
I'm sorry to say "Good-bye"
like this

I've been drafted—I can't go and
don't want you involved

Please go to Nantucket clean out my place
Drop off
the keys, library books
I don't know—
It's a mess—stuff
in the fridge
Say "Thanks" for me

Tell Dad I made it out to Altar Rock—
that I'm sorry

Love Fred

The Letter Received

What is not there:

When did you ever write

"Dear Mother?"
It was: "Folks," "Dear People"
or "Ma & Pa"

No mention of CO status
or of the friend who'd gone
to Canada

None of your macabre tongue-in-cheek
jokes, no puns

No reference to books
(you were always reading)
none of your own books

No odd asides, no rambles to nowhere
or somewhere, no speculations
peculiar comments

Except the reference
to Altar Rock

Not "Muchness," "Love F"
Or the alone
                    "F"

The FBI

Day and night for weeks and months, grey FBI men
watch the house and wait for you. They track
all who come or go with names,
times, dates, calls; and pick through the trash.

They park in a dark sedan on the side street.
They ring the bell. Sit on the couch. They
take notes, read your letter. They ask
questions, interrogate the neighbors and friends.

They walk the campus, drink coffee and question
random students. Our folks know nothing
continue to teach their classes, collect the mail.
They buy food and repeat—they know nothing.

Neither the questions nor the answers change.
Finally they stop.

Alone
in a small
slope-ceilinged
room

the window open
to sky
and chimney pots
you watch

a ginger cat
walk the gutter up
and over
the steep roof

in and out
of windows on his
morning
and evening rounds

Muchness & LoVeM

Stone

Again leaves fall, rain on the old river
on marsh grass

Elm leaves float—swirl
over the clear pebble bottom

Before the mill others came
to pick berries and fish the speckled trout

I am sunk here among lost coins, arrowheads
in the mud of rotting leaves

The water flows
winter cycles winter

Again Orion
appears in the chill air

At the bend in the river two promise
to hold each other

A soldier leans on the rail as water pours
above the dam

He stares long into water
again fog rises off the river and leaves fall

Journey

After cups of Turkish coffee
a rug changed hands crossed deserts and seas

Time past—a child crawled from pattern to pattern
feeling its rough threads on knees and hands

Following the trail left by worn fingers
of earth and sky—woven together

The child's hands marked the sun's path
across ancient colors scattering wordless songs

Following the shifts in shades of blue
he traced its pattern—traveled back

Through twisted streets where muezzins called
and cloaked shapes vanished—back where under an olive tree

Two soldiers slept on a sprung car seat
and children licked ice creams

After cups of Turkish coffee—deep pain exploded
spewed up—ate sleep, walls—ate dreams

The End Game

In the sun's glare off the glass towers she sees fire flash—
Father and child flee from the smoke to the river. On the corner
Four mounted figures wait. She slips through the gate
Under the vaulted ceiling, lights candles—a wisp of prayer against
The coming night. She has seen the signs.

Out of the desert sun, young men meet. Their words echo
The old woman's vision of the end that will fall
In a fierce rain, turning sand and streets red
Under the blazed sun. From the city towers the rooks caw.

The setting sun glares red off the windows, blinds the watchers, busy
They gather and sift the data. In Central Park the air
Does not stir—the pond gives back the trees
And towers. Afraid, the old woman prays for the bearded man,
The skipping child. The end of day.

Five

Begin With the Given

The news lists the death of a child asleep with his teddy,
his mother and father separate in grief;
lists the out-of-work, the kid with a grin, the fruit seller
who lost his cart, the old, the young, anyone;
lists the addict sprawled on the floor, his friend who tried
to help. Lists those who flee
their homes, for life is conquest, war, famine and death.

She wants to stop her ears, to not hear, would keep them all safe
in a place where knives do not cut, fire burn.
She walks through the night hands outstretched, reaches
for walls, cars, people, something.
Toes feel for the edge between road and grass.
She sits on a bench, watches
a bird collect twigs, feathers, strands caught in a thorn bush.

Faces

On a cold February day, I wake to knocking. Scramble-headed,
I step into the hall, the door slamming behind me.
A man descends the stairs, his camel coat flapping.
He tears my sweater, smashes my face. I grip his arm, fight
for my unborn baby. I can't breathe. I fall. He slugs me
again and again. *Don't get blood on my coat.*
I'm locked out. In the silence, I sob. Blood splashes on the rug,
the door, the snow—cold through socks.
The street is still; I slip on bricks.

The corner florist grips my arm, intent
on gathering bright flowers. She seeks the rush of disaster,
collects the news of others' pain.

In the vaulted courthouse down brown corridors, a rush of feet.
Groups cluster, merge and shift. Mothers on wooden benches
wait. *Tell your story to the judge.* I hold my breath,
talk to his hands; my hands hold me up. I cry. He sets the date.
It is cold. I wait in the women's detention room.
Behind chicken wire the matron picks and scrapes varnish off
her desk. We meet again in court.
I stand in the dock, prop against the rail.
Again and again, *Yes, that is the man.*
Are you certain? Will you point him out?
Yes. I am certain. I saw him.

Months later I see him out on bail. I freeze. Nights I cannot sleep.
The story replays and I see the man filming my bruises, the nurse, cops
the grey-haired judge, my father, mother, my love—all
whose skin hurts with my bruised and battered face,
who walk about a mass of quivering nerves
and see my pain as their own.

My baby is born. There is no trial; he has left town. Now I look
at faces, so many with bruises like mine, or wake
with the leftover taste of fear in my mouth. Sometimes out walking
with my little girl, a man of a certain age and look approaches.
I freeze. He comes toward us; my heart bangs; I can't
breathe as he stops to make funny faces with my little girl.

Mud Pies

"People eat dirt in Haiti." —*Boston Globe,* January 2008

He knew he'd need to apologize send flowers, something
to everyone
for fleeing his Welcome Home

But he couldn't smile, eat—
more cake
He had tried to

Alone in a café
he stirs his coffee, stares
at the lights

> *but the people keep coming*
> *his hands keep setting bones, removing bullets*
> *stitching and holding*
>
> *under a tree, shaded from the hot sun*
> *a woman mixes and stirs dirt, water, shortening and salt*
>
> *children watch*
> *she carefully places the mud pies on a board to bake in the sun*
> *later they will eat*

A child in her stroller laughs, shatters his thoughts
he watches her eat, crumbs scattering
carefully she picks one

She studies the man, offers him the crumb
he holds out his hand
she stares and places the crumb in his hand, *Eat* she says

Deep Water Rigs Pump

It is early and there is only the sound of rain
through the open window—

Rain as puddles grow—rain
on the leaves of the oak and on panes of glass. The sound

Is steady, it swells, quiets and drops. The water's rising
each day dirt vanishes—the size of a football field.

In Louisiana there's an island that shrinks. Long ago
the people were driven downriver—

For generations they walked to their burial ground—
they sang and remembered. But now the dead come close.

Upriver the levees hold the water back from fields and towns
no longer does the silt wash down to the delta.

No longer is the marsh renewed. With each storm gulf water floods
the canals cut through the marsh.

The receding water leaves behind salt. In the dirt the trees die
their roots no longer hold fast the ground.

Speak

Of the courage of those who do not pretend
that all is well

Of those who labor
whose hands and feet move in sleep

Of the shadow figures who shuffle endless streets
past storefronts and vacant lots

Of those who sit with the suffering, days stretch
through the night—cool cloths soothe, but do not heal

Of the one million in the Diaspora from the lower 9th
of the five hundred thousand families displaced

Speak of the stubbornness of an old man
yet again—laying tile in an intricate pattern

Everybody living in different places
All scattered, nobody together—but I ain't about to leave

They Have Gone

Under the canopy of trees we feel safe

But a scene replays
endlessly
running back before that moment
when in bright rain they stepped out—
a momentary loss of footing
before the slip
from life to none

It is perhaps a breath, a charm
that holds the twisting vines bridging the chasm

Stop. Rewind back before that instant
hold them close:
the soldier
the student turning pages and the others
as city walls vanish in rubble
leaving painted, twisted stairs
to nowhere

For the Deported

In the early mist the river
surrounds the city
with silence

I breakfast on the bridge
and watch the crumbs scatter
to the water beneath

On the Seine firemen
play their hoses
flooding water back into the sky

I enter the cathedral
in a corner a woman sits
dust and scaffolding enclose her

I carry her silence as I walk
on the street that begins and ends
with the river

There is a man sweeping with twigs
by the fountain women meet
their string bags bulge with fruit

I walk through the city and remember
those who were taken
their words etched on stone

Beyond the scarred wall
a log floats
it is quiet now the light glistens

Under bridges the barges move
and beggars sleep
in silence

A Sense of Place

A woman wept. Her eyes ran rivers and washed
away the dirt from under the oak.
In early morning quiet
mother-in-law and the birds whispered together
they cried, *You must travel the world from house to house.*
She wiped her tears and swept the floor.

Dig through the floor of any house, there in the dirt—fragments
shards of pots, bottle caps, bones, odds and ends, and here—
arrowheads.

Within a single season her footsteps wore a path
from the fields and barn to the kitchen door
sparrows and field mice came.
Beyond the fields and orchard are gravestones
for in spring the river overflowed.
She weeps for those buried in wild grass and brambles.

Six

Think Past the Answer

I

If a door opens
>In an attic someone spins gold thread from spider straw.
>Enter a punch card—the Jacquard
>looms clack and crash.
>Its spools whirl the dance of warp
>and woof, faster than eye or hand—the cloth flows.

Is it tall
wrought iron
>Beyond the city at the edge of cracked asphalt, fire burns
>white hot. Iron rods glow orange-
>red, plunged
>in water they hiss. A man pounds
>iron curls—a filigree of lace for window, gate or door

carved out
from rock
>Though tree-covered hills ring the bay and old leaves
>are thick on the ground, earth is thin
>over gray granite.
>Each year men quarried the stone
>shipped it down the granite rail to the river.

Is it shut
against
>Those that prowl the ghost streets under the overpass
>slip through small chinks into
>empty rooms
>to fashion a world and escape
>the sleet that coats iron rails. Until—late August

the scorch
of sun
>Spills on a man asleep, gilds particles of dust. Enter
>the code: 0 + 1 over and over. Mind
>does not grasp
>the simple language. On Stone
>Mountain, an old man listens and questions

2

By the fountain
> They meet as if by accident—here water flows on birds
> and children splash. They do not
> remember
> the days without rain—
> the choke of fear that crops will shrivel and animals die.

Does the air

move
> With the scent of rain for the parched lands as walls ring
> with the clamor of bells and the cries
> of the people?
> In too bright sun they follow the roads
> through a cloud of dust to the edge of the waterless lake.

Does the dog

turn
> At their approach does he blink and wake from the hunt
> to face the unexpected hand's
> sweet caress or
> lash of rage? In a far courtyard
> a man cuts back roses and calls to the travelers

Can you rake

the stones
> That surround the fountain and create a path for the still
> mind? The fine gravel swirls under
> boxwood hedges
> under the feet of the dog
> and of those who rest on stone benches out of the sun

Can you listen

to water?

Ride the Groove

We tell stories to make sense
of where we are
that was not part of the dream

     Once biking through Rotterdam
     whistles blew
     and through factory gates
     thunder of clogs and cycles hurtled
     in the throng my bike wobbled into a tram track
     stuck in the rut I pedaled

The past stalks me
I wander this city never quite settling
camping out in borrowed rooms

     I watch messengers chain their bikes to street signs, fences
     anything as they ride the city—out on the edges
     taunting trucks, cabs, buses, to give the right of way

Sleepless I listen for the surreptitious footfall
for the closed door to twitch open
I hold my breath

     I would ride
     feet, wheels and streets vibrate
     as sights, sounds explode lights change
     in a whirling assault
     of metal—Music shakes my core

Can I catch its beat?

On the Common the trees are green and newly soft pointillism
these points of color merge to a green bench
where a man speaks,

     Do not be afraid to meet others riding hard

Listening to *Joyful Noise*

Coltrane with Eric Jackson and Leonard Brown

Out of a burst of sound and rhythm, the stars tumble together, streak
and roll down the sky. Great thunder and wail. Sound rips the air

August light flashes over the night grass as children chase
fireflies. They spin and spin, dizzy they flop on grass, stare into
black sky, half asleep they watch a shower of stars. One child sleeps.

Stars fall over her feet in the dark, night stretches. The grass
gathers, the sky drops down to black grass, stars run through trees,
children hold jars to catch the glint of air, song of fireflies and stars.

Out of a burst of sound and rhythm, a horn blows joy over grief, sound
floods, stars tumble together, streak and roll down

Revel in the City

At the light a truck idles
a radio pulses
                Breathe
                in the wild end
                      of a jazz run

In the park a breeze whispers the grass
the leaves—a woodpecker drums a dead branch
                Strain
                to hear the gaps
                      between sounds

Under the cries of children and of fountain song
discordant lovers quarrel
                Listen
                for the quiet
                      in the rhythm

On the walk a girl twirls and dances to the beat
no one else can hear
                Seek
                the space
                      around the echo

Imagine the sounds, words—beneath chatter
beneath thought
                Find
                the pause—the music
                      in the silence

Come, He Said

Clear shimmer
of lake
blue toss of sky

Drops of light
splash

Small black beetles
row
for the far shore

Under the glint
of dragonflies
turtles snap
as frogs doze
among

          White water lilies

Here long
fierce roots
anchor
stalks that break
the surface

As unseen toes quest
fearful
of lost sticks

Puff of black
ink rises

Ooze of muck
and half dissolved
leaves

Out in the middle a loon dives in flat water
on the bank a woman watches
for the bird

Branches surround her, tangle of roots and sky
dissolve into mountains and lake

The day flows—wipes away reflections
dreams blur

Is it too late to surface far from shore
motionless
as clouds shadow the sun

Old Men Say, *Only Earth Endures*

on Katahdin the woods are quiet
far off—a bird

the trail twists through firs
sweet ferns

over fallen logs
sheer rock

at Chimney Pond

out from trees a moose and her young
drink knee deep

from their mouths
drops fall

Point No Point

"Great joy in camp," Clark wrote in his journal. "We are in view
of the ocean, this great Pacific Ocean which we had so long
anxious to see." —A spiritual journey around the coast of
Washington.

She left Seattle for the Edmonds Ferry; diesel and salt fog the air;
gulls shriek, the horn blasts, the rope slaps; there's a bump
and squeak of hull on pilings;

Back and forth; horns and halyards are muffled in the continual drip.
      She stares through the wipers' rhythmic ark
      at the sweep of lights in fog.
She drove toward Point No Point Lighthouse, built in 1879. Signed away

By the defeated Chimacum, Skokomis and S'klallam tribes. Seen as
      a "long nose" or guardian rocks—
      The oldest light on Puget Sound
marks a mud flat once thought to be a deep channel.

There are many birds off shore and in the tidal marsh: gulls,
cormorants, terns, jaegers, ducks, grebes, scoters;
when the tide is running there is a feeding frenzy.

She stopped for coffee with muffins then more coffee; she drove under
soaked trees past naked hills of stumps, a hawk; a girl and her dog.

In La Push the waves roll, beat on the sand—the hard sand as the sun
      slants through dark clouds and people walk the beach.
      A wolfhound and small black dog attack the surf.
Blackberries grow amid silver, upended trunks, roots of ancient trees.

In the harbor firs ridge the sea stacks—twist of trees, stark against the
      grey sea. Chilled she feels the sea thud
      repeat against the sand; below
the cliffs bright anemones and starfish shine in the silver wash.
At Quileute a diesel roar as men race canoes in the shelter of the jetty;

Their families cheer, sell smoked salmon, silver, homemade crafts,
Twilight goods and re-live the past.

On the road she drove through rain till dark; slept in the truck to all
night rain that drummed then sputtered and stopped.

In Westport the tide is out. At water's edge a long line of birds; a fog
        horn blows counterpoint to the waves;
        hooded figures pace;
a raven stalks across grey sand, steps through driftwood; sharp grass
covers the dunes.

From within a shelter of tree bones, she hears the surf rumble; tries to
        imagine that fear blows before the wind;
        that under clouds
she might laugh at the spatter of rain, meet the surfers on the beach.

Spin, spin ragtag thoughts tumble head over heels, re-align upside
with down, and chase through the Scotch Broom over the dunes.

She drove past iron sculptures. The flat cutouts of bear, moose, deer,
        egrets stalk the harbor, march past mountains of oyster shells. She

drove the repeating hills, past fish weirs, past wading birds. In Long
        Beach she drove on packed sand
        just out of the waves' reach;
red-gold, multi-colored kites twist and toss in grey sky over grey sand.

Her tangled thoughts tug to be free. Within a café she sips coffee. Far
        from the sound of wind or sea,
        she dreams in the glow
of light under a wagon wheel, as bone antlers, heads stare at nothing.

Something drives her back on the road. Perhaps it was the sound of
tires; perhaps it was the light on grey water and rocks; or the owl
awake on his branch. No words can measure the depth of his eyes.

In Ilwaco tourists crowd the Harbor Walk shops and booths: they
nibble smoked fish, cranberry bites, try on fancy hats and shirts
       create memories, photos
       of time set free;
they collect remnants of the Peninsula's near-forgotten past.

The day lingers on sellers, fishermen, sightseers.
       She drove to Cape Disappointment Lighthouse,
built in 1856 at the mouth of the Columbia River—destination of
Meriwether Lewis and William Clark. She climbs the lighthouse

stairs, echo of feet and tumult of voices in the metal tower.
It was the end of the road. Then as now gulls cry and waves crash.

The Lady Is Changed

by the breath, flute of bird. As the stars dim she takes off her skin
crosses wet grass to the lake and weeps.

She is the one with grey dreads by the overpass, the one who whispers
made-up songs of yellow flowers and paints gaudy lions.

She shows a child the rings of a tree stump, the wide ones signifying
rain and sun the thin ones a dry hard year.

She dreams the past a threshold.
On the water it is raining. Loons dive and call.

Ω

Acknowledgments

These poems were first published in the following publications, some in slightly different versions:

Bagel Bards: "Ride the Groove," "*Come,* He said," "Caught Unaware," "News of the Day"
Constellations: "Stone"
Ibbetson Street: "Revel in the City," "For the Deported," "Dream Catcher," "Deep Water Riggs Pump," "Night Visitations"
Knock: "Slowly Leaf by Leaf"
Off the Coast: "Mud Pies"

Supportive Friends and Readers: Gabrielle Bachmeier, Elizabeth Bennett, Mary Buchinger Bodwell, Martha Collins, Bernadette Davidson, Harris Gardner, Danielle Legros Georges, Fred Marchant, Louisa Solano, Kathleen Spivack, Brian Turner, Patricia Yingling, The Bagel Bards, The William Joiner Institute Writers' Workshop, The Writing Group at United First Parish Church.

Cover artwork, artistic treatment by Diane Kistner of a photo of Point No Point by the author; cover and interior book design by Diane Kistner; PT Serif text with Gill Sans titling

About FutureCycle Press

FutureCycle Press is dedicated to publishing lasting English-language poetry books, chapbooks, and anthologies in both print-on-demand and Kindle ebook formats. Founded in 2007 by long-time independent editor/publishers and partners Diane Kistner and Robert S. King, the press incorporated as a nonprofit in 2012. A number of our editors are distinguished poets and writers in their own right, and we have been actively involved in the small press movement going back to the early seventies.

The FutureCycle Poetry Book Prize and honorarium is awarded annually for the best full-length volume of poetry we publish in a calendar year. Introduced in 2013, our Good Works projects are anthologies devoted to issues of universal significance, with all proceeds donated to a related worthy cause. Our Selected Poems series highlights contemporary poets with a substantial body of work to their credit; with this series we strive to resurrect work that has had limited distribution and is now out of print.

We are dedicated to giving all of the authors we publish the care their work deserves, making our catalog of titles the most diverse and distinguished it can be, and paying forward any earnings to fund more great books.

We've learned a few things about independent publishing over the years. We've also evolved a unique, resilient publishing model that allows us to focus mainly on vetting and preserving for posterity poetry collections of exceptional quality without becoming overwhelmed with bookkeeping and mailing, fundraising activities, or taxing editorial and production "bubbles." To find out more about what we are doing, come see us at www.futurecycle.org.

The FutureCycle Poetry Book Prize

All full-length volumes of poetry published by FutureCycle Press in a given calendar year are considered for the annual FutureCycle Poetry Book Prize. This allows us to consider each submission on its own merits, outside of the context of a contest. Too, the judges see the finished book, which will have benefitted from the beautiful book design and strong editorial gloss we are famous for.

The book ranked the best in judging is announced as the prize-winner in the subsequent year. There is no fixed monetary award; instead, the winning poet receives an honorarium of 20% of the total net royalties from all poetry books and chapbooks the press sold online in the year the winning book was published. The winner is also accorded the honor of being on the panel of judges for the next year's competition; all judges receive copies of all contending books to keep for their personal library.

www.ingramcontent.com/pod-product-compliance
Lightning Source LLC
Chambersburg PA
CBHW070008100426
42741CB00012B/3158